Beyond Racism

D1519019

Beyond Racism

A Deeper Understanding
of Cultural Diversity

Verlene Grant

KIRK HOUSE PUBLISHERS
Minneapolis, Minnesota

Beyond Racism
A Deeper Understanding of Cultural Diversity
by Verlene Grant

Cover design by Jesse Hubard
Illustrations by Daniel Barsody
Editors: Tricia Van Ee, Nancy Michael

Library of Congress Cataloging-in-Publication Data

Beyond racism : a deeper understanding of cultural diversity / Verlene
Grant
        p.cm.
   ISBN 1-886513-39-2
        1. Multiculturalism—Poetry. 2. Ethnic relations—Poetry. 3. Race
relations—Poetry. 4. Racism—Poetry.

PS3607.R367
811/.54—dc22

                                                    2004054827

Kirk House Publishers, P.O. Box 390759, Minneapolis, MN 55439
Manufactured in the United States of America

Acknowledgments

There are many angels that illumined my path and made this book possible. I would like to thank each of you from the deepest level of my heart.

To Patrick Henry Grant Jr., my soul mate. Without you, this book would not have been written. Thank you for being the alligator that bit away the unreality in my life so I could see the truth, know the truth, speak the truth, and live in the truth. You are my greatest gift in this life. Your courage, strength, passion, wisdom, understanding, and love have taken me beyond limitations into a whole new world of unlimited possibilities.

To Oliver and Sadie Byers, my dad and mom, the two beautiful souls that gave me life and showed me it was easier to love than to hate. You taught me to choose the higher way and you led by example. Your commitment to God and family gave me a strong foundation. Thank you.

To the MCARI (Minnesota Churches Anti-Racism Initiative) team. Thanks for believing in me and giving me the opportunity to work with you and learn about the systemic nature of racism.

To Margie, my sister, who made her transition from life earlier this year. Your life and suffering taught me much. You were right, "time is precious and must be used wisely."

To God, my teacher, my inspiration, and my best friend, thank you for showing me a better way.

*Dedicated to all the great Spirits
who have risen above man's inhumanity to man*

Contents

Prologue

Where are we in our quest for human justice? Times have changed, laws have changed, and yet we still struggle with how we will get along as human beings in a world full of diversity. We invent rules of engagement and then break them as soon as there is a threat of loss of power and control. Racism represents the breaking of a fundamental rule of existence for humankind. It separates and threatens to destroy all that life stands for.

Racism—will it ever go away or is it here to stay? In the United States, racism continues to exist because it is still profitable for some to thrive at the expense of others. The reality is that we are all affected by racism. Like an insidious cancer that is ignored or left un-treated, racism remains as one of the most destructive forces in the world and has begun to snuff out the life of our thriving society.

Most of us are ready to move beyond racism. There is a hunger within us, a desire to connect and experience the bountiful gifts that diversity brings. We are the silent majority. Yet we are beginning to exercise our collective power to eradicate racism. We are ready to see a new day where all people are treated fairly with respect and honor, for just being part of the human race.

We are not willing to wait any longer; rather, we will be the catalysts for change that sets the stage for future generations to live in harmony together as one.

Some say that I am a dreamer, but I am not alone. There are many that think as I do and are willing to step forward to create change in their corner of the world.

However, some of us are not sure how to get started. So we wait for the right plan or direction, and then we act.

Our challenge is to continue to stay focused on what is right, what is just, and what is truth in an era where power matters more than justice. Those who insist on participating in racism will soon struggle alone left to deal with the consequences of their inability to embrace truth, peace, and love.

Life is simple, but it has been made complicated by illusion. Racism is born of illusion, and it is truth that will shatter its very existence. What is real, what is truth, will always prevail.

Beyond Racism is designed to evoke deep thought and raise more questions than answers. And the answers you seek are within you. If you will sit with the conflict that arises, *Beyond Racism* will ignite the truth that is within and bring us closer to each other, and our Source.

As we begin to understand the nature of illusion in relation to truth, we can see deeper into the illusion that created racism and how it is being sustained by the *man's truth* of power, belief, and resistance. There is no law greater than the Law of Truth. If we know the truth, we can be free from the barriers that keep us bound to mediocrity and a continual web of unreality.

There can be no freedom without truth, for truth is the foundation of the existence of human life. Remember?

There is a place beyond racism
let us meet there!

Chapter 1

All Are Not Created Equal

Individuality

The concept that *all men are created equal*
is designed to cover up the *real* truth and measure
everyone according to a standard created by the dominant
culture, which by its nature is separatism.

All are created as a unique expression of the Creator.

Certainly all are not created equal in potential,
awareness, or ability.
All do, however, have the capacity to grow into their
own life design.

If equality means sameness, it is not an attainable goal.
No two snowflakes are alike, so it is with mankind.
The condition of being different is the nature of life
and different does not mean equal.

We will never be the same; that is not our design.
What is attainable is removing barriers and limitations
that prevent one from reaching full potential.

Individuality is the One divided into the all.
To focus on equality and not on individuality
is a setup to exclude one that is different.

Belief

Racism is a belief system.
We believe in superiority and control.
We believe in a system that renders unfair justice.
That is why acts of racism, whether covert or overt
are often overlooked and accepted by most as normal
behavior.

Racism limits and controls individuality.

To place limits on others and get them to believe
in those limitations creates a barrier that can only
be broken by death or truth.

Racism is a false barrier and only works when fed
by individuals that give it power through belief.

Racism, created by belief, can be destroyed by truth,
if we believe.

Structure

Structure gives form to our lives,
like temperature gives form to water.
When we place structure above individual potential,
we create an unhealthy condition that is paralyzing.

Equality is a structure designed to limit individuality.

In our current structure of systems and institutions
is there really *equal opportunity* for all?
I think not.
The structure of *equal opportunity* was
created by the dominant culture
as a way to sustain the dominant culture.
Equal opportunity is administered by the dominant
culture, taught to the dominant culture,
and all are measured by it's standards.

When individuality supersedes equality the individual
can move beyond structure.
Example:
> A leader emerges in spite of a framework
> designed to oppress and suppress the
> inherent ability to fulfill her destiny.

Destiny's seed is found in individuality.
Structure prevents maturation.

Chapter 2

To Be or Not to Be

Being

The state of being is wholeness.
The quality of being is integration.
The nature of being is harmony.

Being human is a process of evolution
from duality (both human and divine)
into individuality and returning into duality again.

The in-between life experience is what determines
our next step in evolution.
The process between individuality and duality
is relationship.
Being human has to do with how we relate to others
in the state, quality, and nature of *who* we are.

What one chooses to be in relation to another
dictates the quality of being for that individual.
Integration creates wholeness and
promotes growth and prosperity for all.

To be or not to be is a moment by moment
decision that shapes individuality
in relation to all of life.

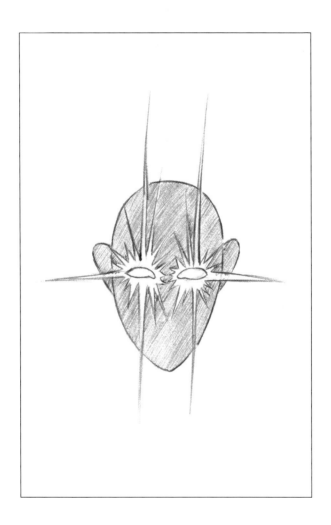

Fear

Fear has the power to both create and destroy.
It creates illusion and destroys the evidence of truth.
It renders its victims powerless and delusional.
Fear causes the individual to experience the illusion of
that which she or he is afraid of.

It has been said that all fear stems from
the "fear of separation."
If this is true, then there is nothing to fear.

The truth is separation exists only in the mind.
We can never really be separated because we came
from the same Source and we are all interconnected
by that Source.

So, we made the whole thing up,
and the fear of separation is an illusion
that has been made real by the mind.

Love cancels out fear.
The courage of the heart can remove fear and
lead to the Spirit of Truth and Love.

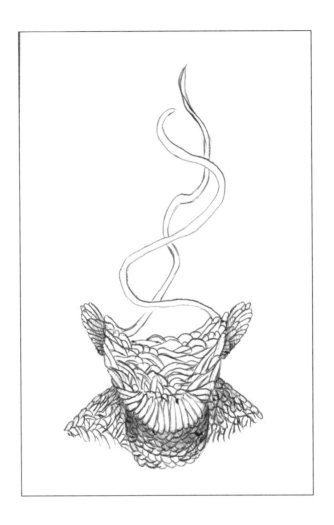

Substance

Substance gives quality to existence.
Difference gives beauty to substance.
Each unique individual adds substance to
the whole garment of humanity, and
diversity is the fabric from which mankind is woven.

Fear is the substance of racism.
Its nature is hate, ignorance, and separation.

However, the substance that divides us can be
eliminated by a substance that is within us.
That substance is love.

We were created from love.
We chose to accept the illusion
of superiority and separation,
which opened the door to hate and fear.
These became the dominant substances
of the dominant culture of racism.

Accepting racism as a way of life
has diminished the quality of human existence.

Harmony

Nature teaches us about harmony.
The elements of air, fire, water and earth coexists in
harmony to support organic life.
Which of these elements can claim dominance?
Is air superior to water or earth to fire?

To divide the human race in order of "superiority"
is like trying to live in the human body without air.
Impossible!

*Racism is a system that divides the human race by placing one
group above another for the purposes of power, control, and
economic gain.*

This system of division disrupts the harmony
of mankind, thereby creating an experience of lack.
THERE IS ENOUGH FOR EVERYONE.
To think otherwise is folly.

In nature, harmony is the seed of abundance.
To experience the abundance of life,
live in harmony with all of life
and life will reward abundantly.

Chapter 3

To Everything There Is a Reason

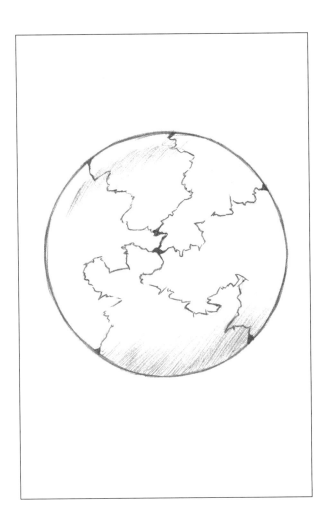

Wholeness

In the coming forth of creation
there existed balance, purpose, and harmony.
Life is a circle without a beginning or ending point.
In the circle of life there is a coming forth and a return.
At this point in time, life is on the return cycle,
gathering together that which was lost in the coming
forth.

The circle of life represents the wholeness of
mankind collectively and individually.
The individual is complete, contained in the One,
made by the One.
All have one breath, all came from the dust, and will
return to the dust again.
That which we have lost through separation,
by excluding others, must be restored
by integrating and creating a condition of wholeness.

Humans have a blueprint for wholeness
which can be found in the family.
There is an adult that brings forth a baby.
The baby becomes a child.
The child grows into an adolescent becoming an adult.
The adult becomes an elder, then returns,
thus completing a cycle of wholeness.

If balance is not achieved, if purpose is not fulfilled, if
harmony is not attained,
the cycle begins again.

A Beginning

In a beginning there were five dominant cultures that
humans defined by skin color and called them "races."
All skin colors were represented as part of each
dominant culture and together they formed a rich
vibrant community.

In the original design of the human race
each culture exemplified a distinct role and quality
as seen in the family structure;
to support a blended, balanced, healthy society.

The red race/culture represented by the BABY = LOVE

The brown race/culture represented by the CHILD = FREEDOM

The yellow race/culture represented by the ADOLESCENT = COURAGE

The black race/culture represented by the ADULT = POWER

The white race/culture represented by the ELDER = WISDOM

If the Elder brings ignorance to the human family,
courage is lost, freedom becomes oppression,
love is replaced by hate, and power turns into apathy.

Society then, becomes a tapestry
woven of hate, fear, apathy, and injustice.

A Symphony

The original culture roles, although
not necessarily seen today, were intended
to blend with the Whole of humanity
creating a symphony, a harmonious sound
that would resonate throughout the cosmos.

Racism destroys the harmony of mankind
creating a dissonant sound
that disrupts the flow of light energy
that is needed to sustain the human race.

The barriers that separate us
must be removed in order to support
life which is prolonged through
balance and harmony.

The key to maintaining balance
is to understand the harmony of integration,
which blends the family of humanity
creating a vibratory action that
pulsates with diversity.

Chapter 4

Man Know Thyself

Creation

The world you want to live in needs you to create it!

You are gods
creating a world for present and future existence.
Every thought, emotion, or deed is a creation
designed to enlighten or destroy.

The world is a giant emulator
of individual and collective;
conscious or unconscious creation.
When love becomes hate, war—peace,
sickness—health, abundance—lack, we created it.

Racism, one of our creations,
separates the souls of mankind to
interfere with the progress of spiritual evolution.

Fed by the mass consciousness of belief,
racism continues to thrive and is alive and well today.
It's destructive nature predicts a future
filled with pain, disease, and death.

The antidote:
>   *Create a world of compassion, hope and acceptance.*
>   *Create a world where the spirit of humanity can soar.*
>   *Create a world where the souls of humanity*
>   *can ascend with complete freedom into maturity.*

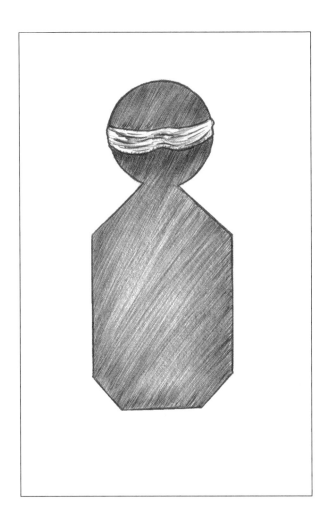

Faith

*Faith is the substance of things hoped for
the evidence of things not seen.*

If faith is lost,
hope is lost also.
When hope is lost,
the meaning of life is lost.

Faith opens the door to truth
and when faith becomes certainty,
it leads to knowledge and understanding.
Truth does not need faith to prove it,
but it does take knowledge to understand it.

Know this: racism is born of ignorance.
Those who participate in it lose intelligence and
drown in a sea of delusion and deception.

Faith is the lifeline to awareness, and
enlightenment ignites the knowledge
to implement a better way.

Spirit

Source is the Light energy of all life.
Its nature is Love.
Its quality is Spirit.

Know yourself as Source knows you.
Formed in Spirit and flesh,
the soul was born.
It is the Source Spirit within each soul
that can bring balance and harmony to the world.

In order to create racism,
man had to disconnect from Spirit,
thereby leaving mankind in a vulnerable state
open to receive energy from a lower source.

A society that participates in racism
incrementally loses Light energy.
Thus its inhabitants can slowly become
the living dead,
having breath but very little Spirit.

Spiritual beings will not participate in racism.

Justice

Where there is no Spirit, there is no justice.
Justice is the correct use of the Law.
The Law of Being is precise.
Sealed in wisdom,
administered by courage, and
upheld with power,
it brings freedom, joy, and love.

Justice is balance.
Where is the balance in racism?

Racism is justified by fear
and implemented by abusive power.
Therefore, it brings confusion instead of order.
Programmed by the dominant culture,
those who are oppressed become the oppressors.
And both have a false sense of what justice is.

The universal Law of Justice
always brings balance,
sooner or later.

Life

Life is a continuous flow of light energy and works best
when all participate together.

There is an order to life.
Notice breath.
The inflow integrates with the outflow,
thus you have a continuous flow of breath.

Life is a balance of giving and receiving,
Yin and Yang.
If one gives more
and the other receives more,
there is an imbalance that creates resentment in both.

In order for humanity to have balance
all are welcomed to participate
in the giving and receiving
of life's many gifts and talents.

Racism creates imbalance and interferes with the ebb
and flow of life.

Chapter 5

There Is a Better Way

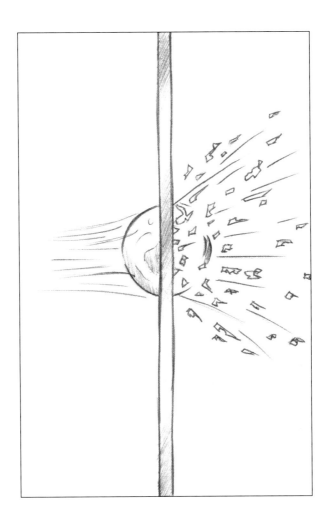

Break It

The saying, *If it ain't broke, don't fix it,*
assumes that the design is perfect.

From one point of view,
a system that gives access to some
and excludes others may seem to work
just fine the way it is.
For others, a fix is in order.

A system built on the foundation
of freedom and inclusion works better for all.

Such a system gives power, opportunity, and
support to all of its members.
It receives peace, abundance, and strength in return.
That system is healthy and balanced.
It is a system created
by the people, for the people.

Break the habit of racism.

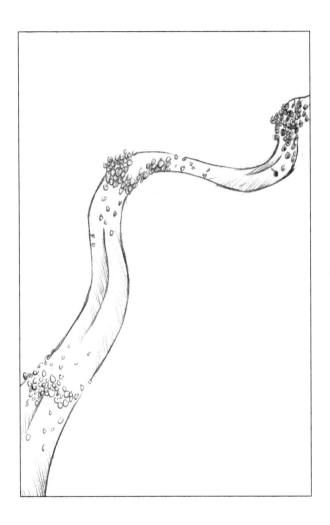

Analyze It

Racism is like a growing cancer
spreading its ills throughout the land and beyond.
Its effect is spiritual and physical disease.

Unless a culture evolves, history repeats itself.

The culture of racism didn't start here in America.
Yet the adversity of racism gives Americans
an opportunity to evolve into a higher culture.

Before this can happen, Americans must analyze
the nature of racism,
who benefits from racism,
why it continues to thrive and sustain itself, and
what must be done in order to eradicate it.

A system that is divided is weakened.
It will eventually crumble under its inferior design.
So, it is enlightened self-interest for us
to figure out how to create a system that is free of racism.

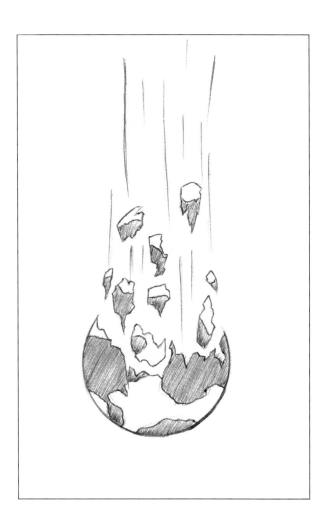

Rebuild It

Racism's bad seeds have infected us all.
We need an antidote
that will bring us back to our basic nature
which is: wholeness, integration, and harmony.

An antidote for racism can be found in the
Five A's of Humanity:

AWAKE   ADAPT   AMEND   AGREE   ADVANCE

AWAKE - *Be fully conscious of who you are, and your purpose of being.*
ADAPT - *Be compatible with the environment; preserve it for future use.*
AMEND - *Correct errors, improving yourself and others.*
AGREE - *Live in harmony together.*
ADVANCE - *Promote a culture of healthy growth for all people.*

A newer generation of enlightened ones
will be taking over soon.
They are not willing to live by the "status quo."
They understand the advantages of being fully integrated.
And, they will build a system that does work for all,
or not.

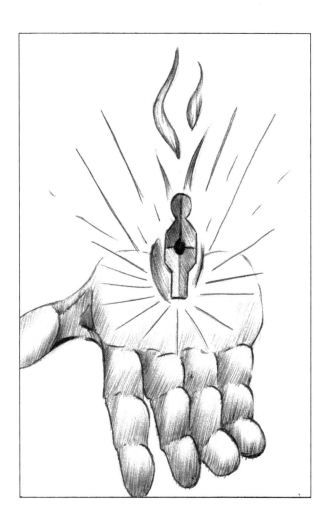

Enlightenment

Enlightenment is the way of an evolved society.

Enlightenment comes to those who are fully awake.
They are the ones
that will bring about change in the world.
They see beyond what their physical eyes behold.
They see within and without, past, present, and future.
They understand cause and effect, and
their actions are carefully ordered.

The enlightened ones are the responsible ones.
It is they who have integrated with the world around them.
Focused on integration,
they use all of life's resources.
They give and receive without limits.
They replenish the earth.

Enlightenment is the nature of Spirit, and
Spirit is the nature of human beings.

Five A's of Humanity

Life is an individual collective journey,
One for all—all for One.
Everything begins with the One and expands outward.
Change individually,
then collectively create a better society.

The *Five A's of Humanity* is a guide for enlightenment
and a statement of being.

- ☯ AWAKE: I am aware. I am aware of myself in
  relation to others. I know reality and live in it. I am
  watchful and conscious.

- ☯ ADAPT: I am flexible. I live with the environment,
  giving and receiving in balance.

- ☯ AMEND: I am willing to improve for the better.
  I continually make right the wrongs that are done.
  I stand for justice.

- ☯ AGREE: I am harmonious. I resolve conflict and
  seize the opportunity it brings. I embrace diversity.

- ☯ ADVANCE: I am progressive. I actively participate
  in raising the consciousness of mankind. I strive to
  grow in wisdom and add value to others and myself.

Chapter 6

The Human Family

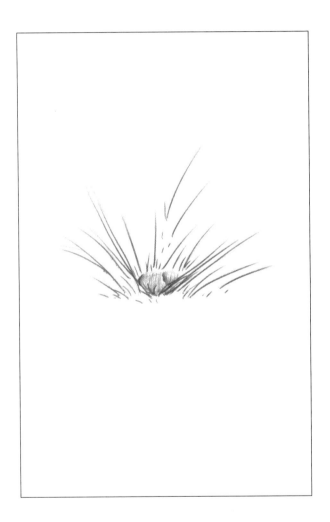

Baby

When is the last time you held a new baby?
Remember the Chi energy?
Pure love in a bundle of flesh
representing the essence of Creation.

The baby, represented by the red culture,
is closest to nature and Spirit.
This culture brings the gifts of joy and love.

Human nature is to love and be loved.
Love is what makes the wheel of life spin.
The nature of earth is to love and be loved.
Unconditional love does not exist.
It suggests imbalance, lack of ebb and flow.
The condition of love is love.

Living within the nature of love
is key to the survival of planet earth.

Love's nature is balance.
Love gives and love receives.
Love demands respect, honor, commitment, and devotion.
Without these, love is not present.

Child

Except you come as a little child,
you cannot enter the kingdom.

The kingdom is a place where abundant life flows
and a little child can show the way.

The child, represented by the brown race,
brings peace, creativity, and freedom to the human
family.

A child's nature is innocence and purity.
The child thrives in freedom and creativity.
It is not limited or restricted.
Pure in thought and simple in heart,
the child expresses harmony and truth.
Unreality is an offense to the child and
shapes a future of deceit, fear, and pain.

Racism is an offense to mankind.

Life is simple.
When the simple life is lost,
deception, lack, guilt, and shame is gained

Adolescent

The adolescent is the fruit of life.

Represented by the yellow culture, the adolescent
brings the gift of courage to humanity.
The adolescent is brave, has honor, integrity,
and pride, is physically strong and intelligent.
Not afraid of a challenge, the adolescent
brings innovation and scientific advancement.

Family and structure are very important to adolescents,
although they tend to display a different external attitude.

Adolescence is a difficult period in development.
Not quite a child and not yet an adult,
they are often confused about their role in the family.
Sometimes they act as a parent and
sometimes they behave as a child.

When the adolescents are not properly nurtured
by strong leadership, love, security, and guidance,
they feel threatened, lost and confused.
Courage turns to fear, fear turns to hate,
and hate turns to acts of violence.

The adolescent is a mirror reflection of the adult and
elder.

Adult

Absent true leadership, the people will follow a derelict.

The adult, represented by the black culture,
brings the gift of leadership and authentic power.
From this culture all others were born.
They represent community in its truest form.
The adult is responsible and therefore most likely
the one to restore family culture.

The seed of the black culture
is integrated into all cultures
and every skin color.
They are identified as those with a strong spiritual base.
They are the natural leaders,
bringing balance, justice, principle, knowledge, and
prudence.
They personify power.
And they are often hated by those in positions of
authority who have not reached maturity.
This culture is an affront to their abusive power.

Now is the time for the adults of this nation
to come forward and take their rightful place as leaders!

The motto of an adult is: "I am my brother's keeper."

Elder

Give instruction to a wise man, and he will be yet wiser.

The elder in the family,
represented by the white culture,
brings the gift of wisdom.
The elder gives wise council, introduces refinement,
provides vision and organization.
The elder shows the children how to cooperate
and use their gifts in harmony with the family.

When wisdom turns to ignorance,
leaders make decisions without
regard to the spiritual consequences.
To be in a position of leadership and
exclude those who naturally possess
the quality of leadership is not wise.

Wisdom shall be the stability of our times.

It is the power of wisdom that sustains the family.
Wisdom satisfies the curiosity of youth,
supports the adult, and provides a strong foundation for
the advancement of the entire family.

.

Reality Check

A balanced harmonious unit has healthy boundaries,
provides leadership, stability, moral values, support,
love, spirituality, and discipline.

A wholesome individual or family
contains all of the components of the family structure—
the baby, child, adolescent, adult, and elder—working
together as one for the advancement of all.

If any one of these are absent, there is a threat to the
stability and function of the unit.

For example, take a look at society today:

Where is the adult influence?
Are the children safe?
Who is teaching values, principles, and responsibility?
Does the adolescent have the family guidance and support?
Where is the love?

There is a breakdown in education.
Children murder their parents.
There is war without cause,
little or no respect for the environment,
improper use of drugs.
We are a materialistic society made up of
irresponsible, selfish, spoiled people.

Chapter 7

Wise Dominion

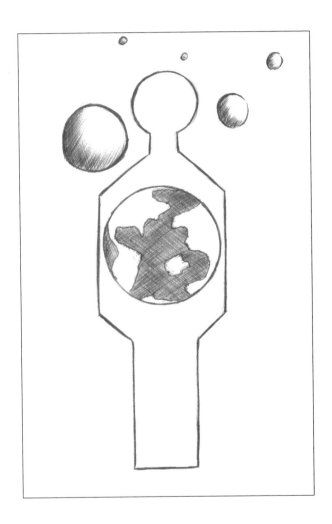

Ego

Ego seals the point of identity for the individual
in relation to the Other.

The healthy ego proclaims:

> *The earth is our kingdom.*
> *Let us reign in harmony*
> *creating a balanced system*
> *that lives by the rules of humanity.*
> *Let us serve the earth and its inhabitants*
> *supporting the growth and fulfillment of all.*

The undeveloped ego claims self – I, me, my.
It lives in fear and hoards resources for its own security.
The unhealthy ego interferes with wise decision.
If ego reigns without wisdom, earth's systems will fail.

Those who are wise integrate ego with Spirit.

The wise ego claims self in others – we, us, our.
It lives in truth and shares resources for the security of all,
multiplying abundance and preserving the earth.

In a society where the wise ego reigns,
each culture contributes evenly, adding value to the
whole, providing enrichment, enlightenment, and
prosperity.

Power

Consider the bully.
It feels powerless,
so it takes power from another.

Now consider also
that the Other has to give up his or her power
for the bully to gain control.
When the Other takes back his or her power,
the bully retreats and is defeated.

Abusive power can never prevail over authentic power.

Abusive power is by its nature power taken from another.
Its very foundation is built on illusion.
Therefore, when faced with authenticity, it crumbles.

Racism's abusive power will not endure
when faced with the authentic power of humanity.

Truth

You will know the truth and the truth will make you free.

It is the nature of man to seek truth.
Truth is freedom, liberation, and power.
Truth and ignorance cannot reside in the same place.
Why? Because one cancels out the other.

Truth is at the core of wisdom.

> *Consider the story of the wise man Solomon and the two women that came to him in dispute. Both women claimed to be mother of the same baby. Solomon ordered that the baby be cut in half and split between the two women. The one that was not the mother said: "Fine let it be neither mine nor yours." The real mother said: "Give her the child." In this story, Solomon used wisdom to determine the truth.*

Ignorance is simply resisting the truth that is within.

Resistance is not the solution to injustice,
for, whatever you resist will persist.
Resistance can only bring more struggles.
The solution is to know the truth and live in it.

Truth is beyond racism.

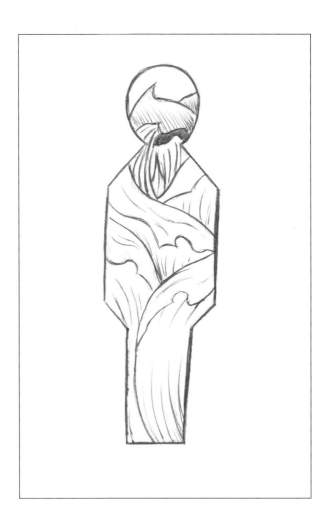

Connection

Humans thrive on being connected.
It stimulates the ego and provides "fulfillment."
However, the focus is usually on external connections:
groups, clubs, organizations, etc.
And these, at best, provide a false sense of belonging
but never really satisfy the void that is within.

Today, many are troubled, unhappy, and empty.
From this state of emotional imbalance
major decisions are made that impact lives and
shape the structure of our systems.

Being inner-connected means connecting the heart
(which is the spiritual center) with the mind and receiving the fullness of love, wisdom, truth, and power.

Connection from the inside—out brings balance.
It integrates the mental, emotional, and spiritual bodies
in harmony for divine purpose
and is the key to happiness.

Inner-connection fills the void, gives real purpose and
value, promotes sound judgement, and
lays the foundation for solid, balanced, productive
relationships.

Relationship

Our first relationship is with Source,
then with self, mother, and family.
From these points of relating,
we learn how to relate with the Other.

If relationship with Source is fear,
relationship with self is insecurity.
If relationship with mother is shame,
relationship with family is guilt.
If relationship with Other is needing approval,
then relationship with self is unworthiness.
And the relationship circle continues.

Racism is born of fear and a sense of unworthiness.
Racist acts are designed to give worth
to one who feels unworthy.

Individual value and worth comes from connection to
Source—which is love.
Love has no fear,
needs no approval,
has no shame, and
has no lack of self worth.

Build relationships based on love not fear.

Chapter 8

Laws of Life

Energy

Energy is in everything.

To act, react, or not act at all uses energy.
Energy is never wasted.
It may be used unwisely, but it is not wasted.
Breath is energy.
Thought is energy.

An allotment of energy is given daily to sustain life.

What an individual thinks or does is recorded
in an energy field and later used to create his or her
world.
So, individual experiences, both negative and positive
are created from his or her storage of energy.

All are interconnected by energy.

Therefore, it is enlightened self-interest
to participate in life by conscious, deliberate action,
that raises self and others to a higher state of advancement.

Misuse of Energy

Man has used an allotment of energy to create racism,
so racism has become life energy—a law unto itself.

The misuse of light energy used to create racism
must be accounted for by those who created it
and live by its law.

The law of racism is designed to
limit the creative power of each culture
so the dominant culture can prevail.

Racism is based on a sense of superiority.
Those who consider others "less than"
have become "less than" themselves.
The very act of racism
has caused them to forget who they are.
They have disconnected from Spirit and
live in a state of inferiority.

Cause and Effect

There is a Law of Cause and Effect
that delivers the outcome that is experienced.

For every action, there is a reaction.
In the cosmos of checks and balances,
all energy is accounted for.

So what is the cause and effect of racism?

The cause of racism is fear and ignorance,
and the effects of racism are dissension,
density, and degradation.
The result, a society of unenlightened people
ignoring the laws of nature and the laws of justice.

Ignoring the law does not liberate one from it.
Becoming the law is liberation.

Understand the Laws of Humanity and become the Law.

The Golden Rule

Remember the golden rule?
Do unto others as you would have them do unto you.

Provided you had a healthy, balanced foundation,
the golden rule works.
But, if you grew up disliking yourself,
thinking you were "not good enough" or
being overly critical of yourself,
your sense of how to relate to others
based on how you relate to yourself is off—track, so
the golden rule is not spirit—based and it does not work.

Racism is based on the golden rule.

Those in positions of power who set the rules of society
do not necessarily have a balanced foundation
based on spirit and truth.
Therefore some of their decisions
are formed in lies, deception, and injustice.
They see the systems that they have created as fair,
giving access to all that "qualify"
according to the "normal" standards created by them.

After all, isn't that what they would want for themselves?

The Platinum Rule

What I do to others, I do to myself.

The quantum theory is based on the concept
that all is part of the One.
And of course this is true.
Also, the Bible talks about *reaping what you sow.*

Both concepts are related in that
whatever one sends out is returned to that one multiplied.
So, if hate is sent to another,
hate returns multiplied by all the hate that
is accumulated in the hate energy field.

Like attracts like.

The same is so if love is sent out.
Love is multiplied by all the love
that is accumulated in the love energy field and returned.
Imagine that.

So whether one acts consciously or unconsciously,
lives within or without the Laws of Humanity,
one will receive the effect of one's actions.

The Platinum Rule is just.
It brings balance to injustice.

Conformity

Be not conformed to this world,
but be transformed by the renewing of your mind.

From the preacher to the president
most of the leaders of this nation teach conformity.
It is easier to follow the crowd
than to act by principle and stand-alone.
It takes wisdom and courage to be a true leader.

Be aware of conformity based on outside programming.

Now is the time for change by renewed thinking.
Follow the Spirit that is within.
Remember the original intention of creation;
then create a new society that is
rooted in higher consciousness,
conformed to a standard set forth by the Creator
and founded in justice and truth.

Chapter 9

America, Grow Up

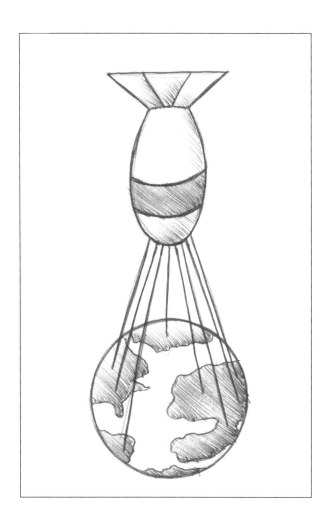

Adolescent Behavior

When courage turns to fear,
war is preferred to peace.

Is America stuck in adolescence?
High crime rates, illiteracy, drug abuse, national
and individual out of control debt,
and, ah yes, racism (including all the other "isms").

Racism *is* <u>unhealthy</u> adolescent behavior.

Why not create an elite system that serves a selected few?
Why not drop bombs on people that don't agree with you?
Why not teach the children to solve problems with violence?
Why not create a justice system that supports the dominant
cultures' self-made superiority?
Why not create poverty and build ghettos?

Why not provide a high standard of education for all?
Why not promote self-sufficiency?

Why not?

A Little Child

And a little child shall lead them.

Life can be confusing because we have forgotten the rules.
The little child remembers.
Observe the child and learn.
Growth and change is a natural part of a child's life.
So the child embraces a simple process for change.

1. The adult or another points out an error.
2. The child recognizes what he or she did.
3. There is a genuine desire to make amends.
4. The child follows instructions and mentally records the results.
5. The child welcomes feedback from others, then adjusts behavior.

Life does not stand still.
If you are alive, you are either growing and expanding or withering and dying.
Change is life and life is change.
Change is inevitable, growth is optional.

Grown–ups forget the simple process of change, thereby making it difficult or impossible to grow.

There is a little child in all of us.
Integrate the quality of the child into adult behavior and choose to grow beyond racism.

Conflict

Conflict is nature's way of creating beauty and growth.
The butterfly, the pearl, the mountain, the stream,
a newborn child—all come from conflict.

With conflict comes opportunity.
If conflict is resisted,
the opportunity is lost.
Strong character is built when
conflict is used as part of the growing process.
When conflict is balanced with wisdom,
it becomes the catalyst for change.

America, a nation born of conflict, is
struggling to grow into maturity.
Her citizens still live in fear,
disputes are still settled with violence,
and exclusivity is a way of life.

Those who have the most to give
are the least accepted by the dominant culture.
Herein lies conflict, thus an opportunity for growth.

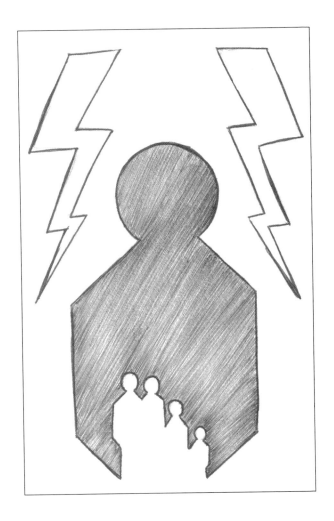

Superiority

The pseudo—role of superiority
can be identified in an unhealthy adolescent
who has lost connection with family and Source.

The state of "being superior"
 is designed to give value to
one that feels of little or no value at all.

The Spirit in all is superior.

Superiority is obtained through spiritual evolution
into maturity.
Maturity comes through integration.
So, those who use racism as a tool to be superior
simply have not grown up.

The superiority complex, born of a feeling of
inadequacy has put this nation
in a potentially dangerous position.
A leader with a superiority complex
is a dangerous force to contend with and
can lead others to death and destruction.

I Am

Everything begins and ends with me.
I am the all of it, the up and down of it,
the in and out of it.
I am responsible for where I've been,
and where I am going.
I live to be – being is who I am.

I am the **joy** of the baby.
I am the **peace** of the child.
I am the **courage** of the teen.
I am the **power** of the adult.
I am the **wisdom** of the elder.

I am that I Am.
To forget this is to live in mediocrity.
To remember is to evolve into maturity and proclaim:

> I am the creator of my universe.
> As I am, so is my experience.
> I create peace, because I am peace.
> I create love, for I am love.
> I create wisdom, because I am wise.
> I create harmony, for I am harmonious.
> I create courage. I am unafraid.
> Because I Am, we are.

The "I Am" of all of us can create a New World, if we
make it so.

Balance

In the history of mankind,
there have been great examples of maturity
embodied in Buddha, Jesus, Gandhi, Mohammed,
Quan Yin.
These individuals represented wholeness.

They reached maturity through
integration and balance.
They became the ALL by becoming the one.
The seed of all cultures was contained within each of them.
Although they may have exemplified one culture or
another, their magnificent gifts of balance
were an example to all.

Examine the lives of these individuals and weigh:
What is out of balance in the world?
What is out of balance in the nation?
What is out of balance in the workplace?
What is out of balance in the family?
What is out of balance in the individual?

Find the answers to these questions and you will find the
keys to maturity.

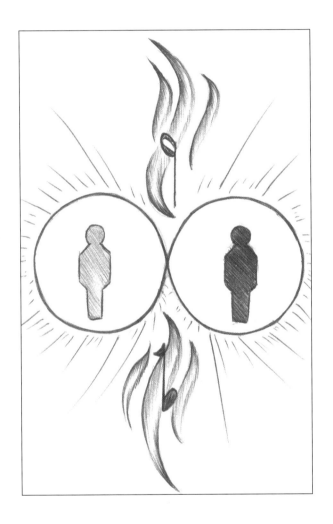

Integration

Integration is the keynote of existence.
Like water seeks its own level, man seeks integration.
For mankind, integration nourishes, enhances,
and provides new life.

Without integration, life becomes stagnated and stale.

The formula of integration is found in wholeness.
With integration, life connects with life,
creating a stream of energy
that feeds into the whole of humanity.
Integration gives opportunity to reach full potential.

A statement of integration:

> I am one with the Great Spirit.
> From the One I expand to the all.
> All that I am is experienced in all of life.
> All of life is experienced in me.

Racism opposes integration
and stops the process of wholeness.
As racism divides,
integration joins together again.
Individual integrated action can be
the beginning of creating a mature society.

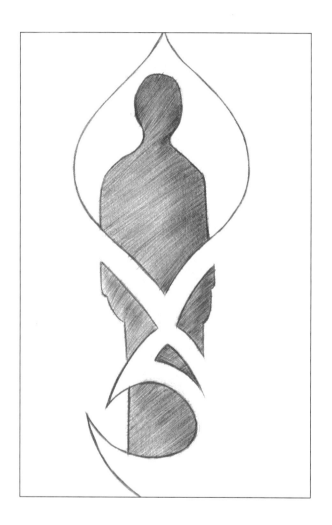

Growth

Life requires growth and change.

Change alone can result in movement
forward or backward.
Growth with change
implies learning, wisdom, or new understanding
mixed with disciplined action that moves one forward.

Growth is the process of shedding off the old
and putting on the new.
Both are essential aspects of mankind's
evolution into maturity.

Change can occur through motivation or inspiration.
Motivation moves from the outside—in and
usually lasts temporarily.
Inspiration comes from the Spirit within
and has the power to create permanent change.

Inspired change is a conscious choice to grow.
Participating in racism
is an unconscious choice not to grow.

Acceptance

To reject the gifts of mankind
is an abomination to life.

All have value and should be appreciated and
accepted as an integral part of the human race.
If America is to advance into maturity,
she must fully accept diversity and learn from all cultures.

No one has all the answers to life's problems.
Together we can create the best solution
for the overall advancement of humanity.

Acceptance does not mean to change the Other
to be as you.
Acceptance means to embrace the Other
as another part of you.

Just as you would not want the head
to look or act like the arm,
so it is with the various cultures of humanity.
Each brings a unique compliment
to the whole body of mankind
and must be received with honor and respect.

Without acceptance, growth is limited.

Chapter 10

Maturity

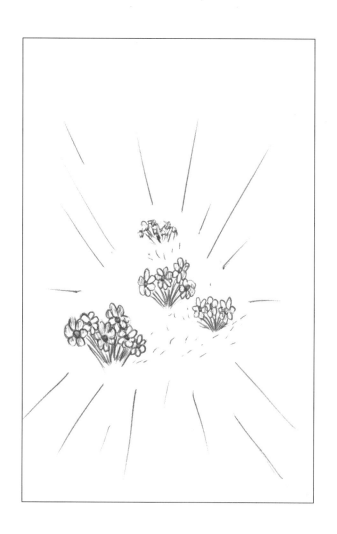

Together

It is normal for humans to live, thrive, and grow together, adding value to the whole of humanity in the process.
Life is a continuous flow of energy.
When we fragment life, we disrupt the wheel of energy and it begins to flow in reverse,
taking life rather than giving it.

As our natural life is taken,
the desire to live becomes intensified,
so the next logical step is to look for life elsewhere.
Therefore we create a tool to sap the life from others in order to sustain our own.
Racism is such a tool.

Taking life from another is not natural and
can only last for a short period of time.
Then life begins to seek balance.

Disease (dis-ease) is formed as a way of creating balance either through healing or removing the infected area.
The diseased life is now snuffed out by a new life which restores balance.

Together we can heal the disease of racism.

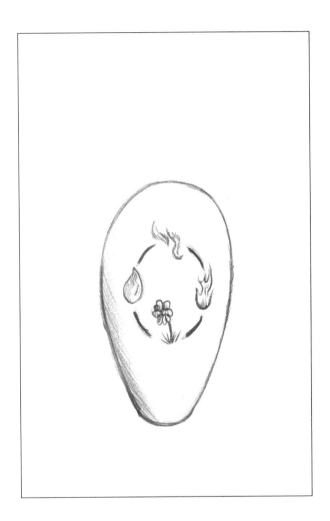

Love

Become reacquainted with love.
Love is not an emotion—it is LIFE.
It is the light energy that formed the earth and all in it.
It doesn't have to feel good or bad.
It just is.

> Love is *air*
> Love is *water*
> Love is *fire*
> Love is *earth*
> Love is YOU

> > Love accepts
> > Love is kind
> > Love is not jealous
> > Love does not boast
> > Love is humble
> > Love is appropriate
> > Love is unselfish
> > Love is calm
> > Love is justice and truth
> > Love is mindful
> > Love supports
> > Love believes
> > Love hopes
> > Love endures

Beyond racism is Love!

Remember

Looking for Love?

Look no further, for the love that you seek is within you.
So you see, everything does begin and end with you.

Humans came fully equipped;
we were formed from God in God,
nothing was missing.
We have it all because
we are a part of it ALL.
The intent of creation is to multiply the ALL.
Remember.

Beyond Racism simply means Re-member
*Bringing all the members of the human family together in
harmony.*

Remember resistance only gives you more of the same.
Notice the natural order of life and flow with it.
After all is said and done,
life concludes with one word: LOVE.
From love I came, to love I will go.

To experience love is to be love.
Remember?

134 • *Beyond Racism*

It Is in YOU

The seeds of the original blueprint
of each culture are within us all.
To be, or not to be, is still the question.
To "be" is beyond racism.
It is full maturity through integration.

Red, yellow, black, brown, or white,
We all have the same stuff—the same base element.

Each of the culture gifts are blended together
into the ONE individual, YOU.
It's in all of us to be wisdom, power, love, courage, and
peace.
So there is no point of separation, for everyone has it ALL.
If you accept and live in integration,
then wholeness is born within you.

When the majority of humanity becomes whole,
the human culture will evolve into maturity.
This is the purpose of life.

Final Word

When it comes to improving the world as you see and experience it, you have the final word. You write the final chapter of your life. And your life does have an impact on the rest of the world. What is your final word?

What is the legacy you choose to leave?

What will you do personally to improve humanity?

How will you implement change?

Author's Note

Both my parents were ordained ministers. My father a pastor and my mother an evangelist. I am number five of six children.

My parents sheltered us from the harshness of life by controlling our interactions with other people. We did not own a television or go to the movies. My mother felt her sole purpose in life was to protect our innocence and to teach us how to live according to God's laws as she understood them. Our parents, as much as possible, tried to shield us from discrimination or at the very least minimize the impact by telling us the truth.

I remember my first encounter with racism. I was around five years old and we were visiting my grandparents in North Carolina. My grandma let me accompany her on a trip into town for business, I was eager to go with her. As we were walking toward city hall, I saw a water fountain and ran to get a drink. Before my grandma realized what was happening, I was drinking. All of a sudden people were yelling and running towards me. My grandma picked me up and ran down the walk. She said sternly: "That fountain is for whites only." I really didn't know what that meant so I asked. She told me that my dad would explain when we got back to her house.

When my father heard what had happened, he said: "Some people are ignorant and think they are better than us. We should just feel sorry for them and love them anyway because we are all God's children."

My parents attitude about racism taught me that
I had the power to create my reality. That is not to say
that I escaped racism, I simply understood that racism
was not as powerful as God. And as long as I was subject
to a higher power, racism would not be the prevailing
factor in my life.

As a family, whenever possible, we challenged
the laws of racism. When my older teenage brother and
sisters rode the bus in the south, they sat in the front
instead of going to the back of the bus. In the early
1950's my dad had a radio broadcast ministry in North
Carolina. For an African American man, that was very
unusual.

At a very early age my parents taught me that it
was normal to have a conversation with God. I, however, thought that it was an exclusive right for preachers.

I remember my dad telling me stories of his talks
with God and the many miracles he experienced in his
life. My mom told me she also had many conversations
with God mostly about raising us. When we lied about
where we were or who we were with, she would say:
"God told me ..." and we were amazed that she was
always right.

My first experience talking to God and getting a
response was in my early twenties. I had moved to
Chicago and decided to explore the wild side of life.
This ended abruptly when I was abducted, beaten, and
almost killed by three men. My plea started in a prayer
and ended in a dialogue. During our conversation, God

quoted a scripture to me and when I asked where it was located in the bible, I got the answer right away. I rushed to validate the information and was thrilled to see the words in the exact chapter and verse indicated. I believe God always talks to us and perhaps a few of us listen. In some of our many conversations, God gave me the insights found in this book.

I am hopeful that all of us will be inspired to choose the higher way of love and eliminate the "isms" that divide us. We can accomplish this if we are willing to change those things that diminish humanity and take us from our original purpose for being, which is to become one with light and truth.

Enjoy the journey.

Verlene Grant conducts dialogues and seminars on Beyond Racism nationwide. She is a consultant, mediator, facilitator and coach. For more information, please contact her at:

PO Box 582295
Minneapolis, MN 55458-2295

www.Beyond-Racism.com